SUPERBUGS

BY EMILY SCHLESINGER

NONFICTION

SADDLEBACK
EDUCATIONAL PUBLISHING
www.sdlback.com

Photo credits: pages 4/5: picture alliance/picture alliance via Getty Images; pages 8/9: Emanuele Cremaschi/Getty Images News via Getty Images; page 11: Jessica McGowan/Getty Images News via Getty Images; page 22: Peter Purdy/Hulton Archive via Getty Images; page 30: akramalrasny/Shutterstock.com; page 31: Ashley Cooper/The Image Bank Unreleased via Getty Images; pages 34/35: Jeoffrey Maitem/Getty Images News via Getty Images; pages 40/41: lev radin/Shutterstock.com; pages 56/57: Pedro Vilela/Getty Images News via Getty Images

ISBN: 978-1-68021-911-1
eBook: 978-1-64598-233-3

Printed in Malaysia

25 24 23 22 21   1 2 3 4 5

Table of Contents

1 Unstoppable

2009

Doctors gather at a hospital. It is in Tokyo, Japan. They are puzzled. A strange goo oozes from a woman's ear. The lab tests a sample. Results show it is a fungus. No one has ever seen it before. They call it *C. auris*.

2012–2013

C. auris begins popping up around the world. It is seen in South America. There are outbreaks across Africa. Infections happen in India. Experts notice something strange. The germ is not being carried to these places. No one is transporting it. Instead, it seems to be appearing out of nowhere. Up to half of the people who get it die.

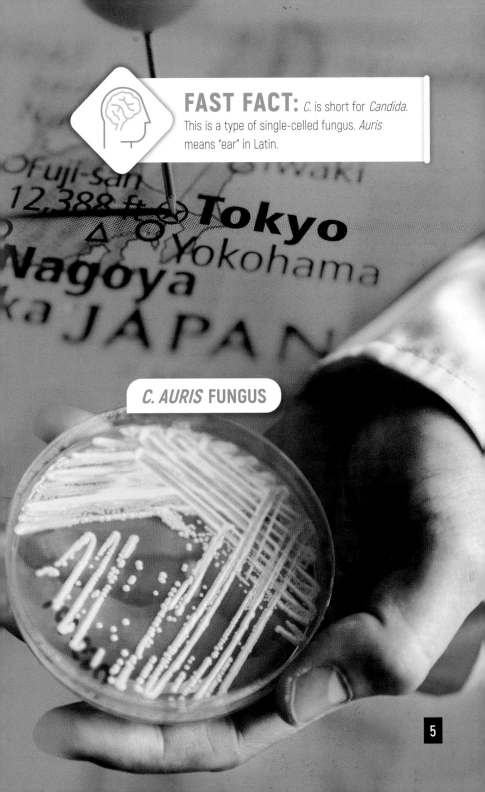

C. AURIS FUNGUS

2015–2016

A hospital in London has a problem. There is a germ going around their intensive care unit. They decide to evacuate. Patients are moved into isolation. Then staff members go to work. Every surface is scrubbed down. Rooms are filled with a gas. This is supposed to kill all germs.

Later, they do tests. Special plates are put out. These collect germs. At first, it looks like everything was killed. Then they look closer. Only one germ remains. Nothing could kill this one. It is *C. auris.*

2018-2019

A man walks into a hospital for surgery. This is in New York. He tests positive for *C. auris*. Hundreds have already been sickened by it in the U.S. Doctors want to stop the spread. They isolate the man. But they cannot save him. Soon, he dies.

They test the room. *C. auris* is everywhere. It is on phones, faucets, lights, and door handles. The fungus hides in breathing tubes. *C. auris* even clings to the curtains.

The hospital has no choice. Ceilings are torn out. Floors get ripped up. Walls are knocked down. Hospital workers will do anything to stop the germ. But they are too late. It spreads to 50 more people. Some say it cannot be stopped.

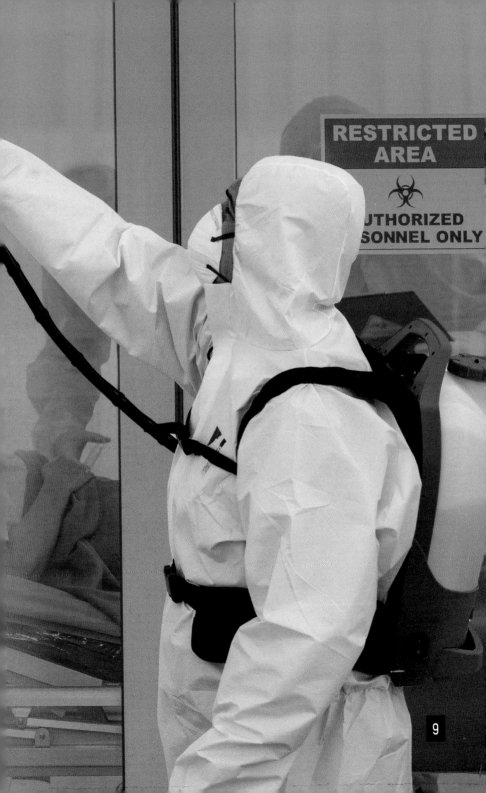

RESTRICTED
AREA

AUTHORIZED
SONNEL ONLY

9

A Powerful Enemy

"This bug is the most difficult we've ever seen." Those are the words of Tom Chiller. He is a health expert at the CDC. Most fungi are not killers. *C. auris* is different. The germ mutated. Now it can live outside of people's bodies. This lets it spread fast. But *C. auris* has an even greater power. It can resist drugs. The strongest medicines do not kill it. That makes the germ hard to stop.

C. auris is not one of a kind. It is part of a growing problem. More and more bugs are acting this way. These are called superbugs. Some are bacteria. Others are fungi or viruses. What makes them "super" is their ability to survive. Most drugs cannot kill them. A few can survive every known drug. This makes them a doctor's worst nightmare.

FAST FACT: CDC stands for the Centers for Disease Control and Prevention. This agency of the U.S. government is responsible for protecting public health.

CENTERS FOR DISEASE CONTROL AND PREVENTION

EDWARD R. ROYBAL CAMPUS

Superbugs are already claiming lives. They kill 700,000 people each year. But the future may be scarier. This number is expected to climb. By 2050, ten million people could die each year. That is more than are killed by cancer.

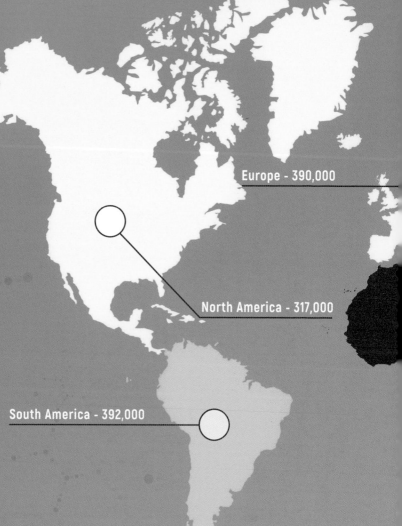

Europe - 390,000

North America - 317,000

South America - 392,000

Projected Yearly Deaths from Superbugs by 2050

Deaths per 10,000 people

5   6   7   8   9   10+

Asia - 4,730,000

Africa - 4,150,000

Oceania - 22,000

Source: Review on Antimicrobial Resistance, 2014

13

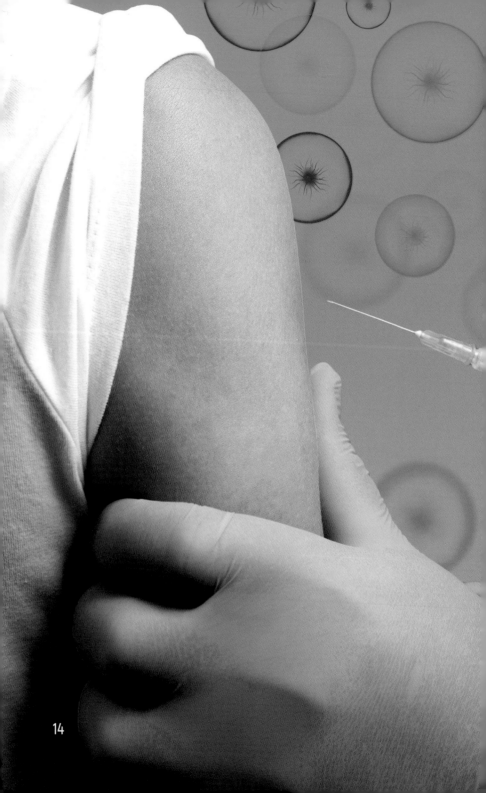

Medicines have gotten better. Science has improved. More drugs are given than ever before. Why would superbugs get worse? Drugs may actually be the problem. We are taking too many.

Bugs are starting to adapt. They are getting used to the drugs. What once killed them no longer does. Many medicines that worked for years now fail. That leaves us without our most valuable weapon.

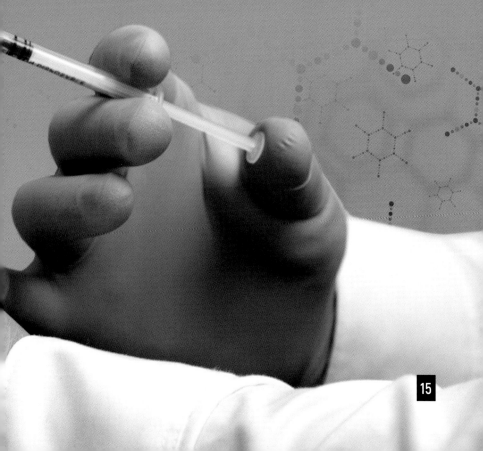

Nightmare Bacteria

It was 2011. A teen went to India. His name was David. He went there to work with orphans.

One day, a train went by. The sleeve of David's shirt got caught. He was dragged with it. His leg got run over. It needed to be amputated.

David came home to the U.S. But his problems were not over. Doctors found an infection. Tests showed a bacteria. It was one they had never seen before.

They gave him antibiotics. These should have killed it. But they didn't. David had a superbug. The hospital carried 19 antibiotics. This germ resisted them all.

A Last Resort

Doctors had a last line of defense. They could give David a rare drug. This might stop the infection. It could also shut down his kidneys.

The risks were big. But David had no other choice. They gave him the drug. His kidneys failed three times. He said it felt like he was dying. Six months passed. David got better. The drug saved his life.

CRE

CRE stands for "carbapenem-resistant Enterobacteriaceae." Carbapenems are a powerful type of drug. Enterobacteriaceae are gut bacteria, or bacteria that live in our intestines.

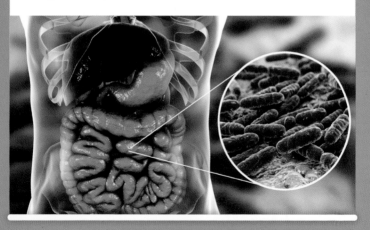

Reno, Nevada

A Nevada woman was not so lucky. It was 2016. The woman had also been in India. She broke her femur. An infection set in. Now she was in a hospital back home.

Doctors ran tests. She had a rare germ called CRE. It was scary even for a superbug. The bug was known to resist the "drug of last resort." This is a medication that can kill almost all germs. But it can also cause other problems when used.

Fourteen antibiotics were tried. None could save her. The woman died. Then the CDC got in touch. They asked for a sample of the germ. Tests were done. Every antibiotic in the U.S. was tried out. There were 26 in all. Nothing worked. The CDC called the bug a "nightmare bacteria."

Antibiotics

For years, antibiotics have kept us safe. You might get a small cut. A nurse puts gel on it. This helps it heal. Perhaps you get a cough. A doctor gives you a pill. The sickness clears up. Both have an antibiotic. It keeps infection away. These drugs may seem like no big deal today. But they once changed the world.

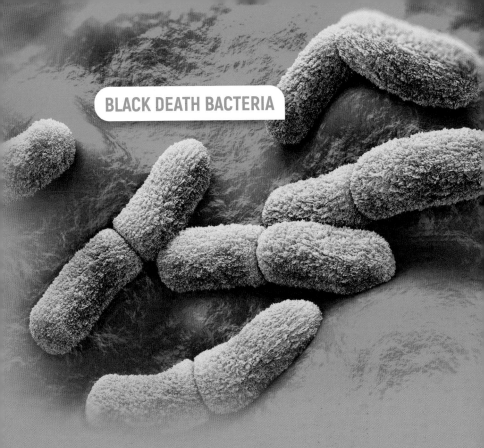

BLACK DEATH BACTERIA

Long ago, life was different. Small cuts could lead to death. Common illnesses did too. A child could get an ear infection. Someone might have a toothache. Back then, these could be deadly.

Some bugs spread around the world. In the 1300s, the Black Death spread fast. This was caused by a single bacteria. It killed 20 percent of the world's population.

A Surprise Cure

It was 1929. Alexander Fleming was a Scottish scientist. He wanted to find a way to kill bacteria. But he was not having much luck. The scientist went on a trip. Then he came back to his lab. Something was wrong. Mold had gotten into one of the dishes of bacteria. Fleming took a closer look. What he saw surprised him. The mold had killed the bacteria.

Fleming knew he was on to something. He turned the mold into a medicine. This is called penicillin. It has saved millions of lives.

ALEXANDER FLEMING

Too Much of a Good Thing

Fleming was proud of his discovery. But he was also worried. The drug might be used too often. Then it could lose its power.

THANKS TO PENICILLIN

Penicillin saved the lives of thousands of American soldiers injured in World War II. Production of the drug ramped up so much during the war that by June 1944 companies were producing 100 billion units of penicillin per month.

The body is like a city. Bacteria live inside. Some are good. Others are bad. They set up "neighborhoods." Good bacteria take up a lot of space. This keeps the bad ones from spreading.

What happens when someone takes an antibiotic? It does not just kill the bad bacteria. Instead, whole neighborhoods are wiped out. Bad *and* good bacteria disappear.

Sometimes a few bad ones remain. These are the strongest. They can survive the drug. Now the bacteria have room to spread. Nothing stops them from taking over the body. Their numbers grow fast. Then they pass drug resistance to their offspring. A gang of superbugs is on the loose.

FAST FACT: Bacteria multiply by splitting in half. They double in number every 4 to 20 minutes. One *E. coli* bacterium can turn into 16 million in just 8 hours.

How Antibiotic Resistance Happens

01 Good and bad bacteria are in the body. A few are drug-resistant.

02 Antibiotics kill bad bacteria that is causing an illness as well as good bacteria.

03 Drug-resistant bacteria are left behind. They can now multiply freely.

04 The bacteria pass on their drug resistance to other bacteria.

Farm Fears

Picture a farm. Thousands of cows line up. They fill a huge barn. Each cow gets a shot. This is an antibiotic. The cows are not sick. Instead, the shot is to **prevent** illness.

Seventy percent of antibiotics are used this way. They are given to animals. This helps for a short while. No farmer wants sick cows. But in the long run it can be dangerous.

FAST FACT: One in five superbug infections comes from food. These include drug-resistant strains of *E. coli* and salmonella as well as CRE.

A Breeding Ground for Germs

Imagine a crowded barn. Animals are close together. They share feed. All drink the same water. Manure covers the ground. Each animal was given a drug. This killed much of their bacteria. But one cow has a resistant kind. It multiplies inside the cow. Then it gets passed to other animals. The bug spreads across the farm.

Scientists did an experiment. They tested meat in supermarkets. What they found shocked them. Most had drug-resistant bacteria.

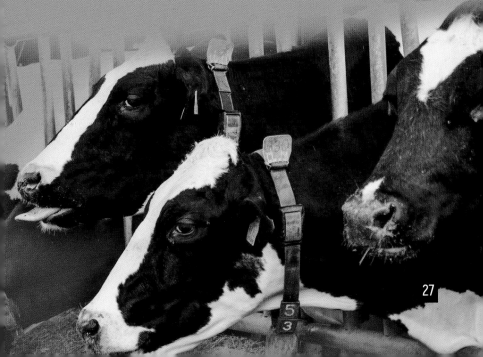

In Our Food

We all have to eat. Should we worry? Most of the time, the answer is no. Cooking kills many germs. Some superbugs do make it into our gut. They usually do no harm. Good bacteria keep them in check. The immune system also helps. It fights them off.

Still, a healthy person may have a superbug. It could live inside them for years. They may never notice a problem.

However, not everyone is safe. Some people have weak immune systems. This is often true for the elderly. Babies are also at risk. People in hospitals might be too. Many are sick. They may have wounds from surgery. It is harder for them to fight off germs.

Experts agree. Superbugs do not belong in our food. Some states are taking steps to keep them out. Laws have been passed. These limit the use of antibiotics. They cannot be given to animals that are not sick. More states may follow. This can help stop superbugs from spreading.

VEGETABLES AND FRUIT

Fruits and vegetables can also carry superbugs. Sometimes animal manure is used to fertilize plants. This can spread harmful bacteria. Pesticides can also be a problem. Many crops are sprayed with chemicals to kill fungi. Over time, these fungi can become resistant to the sprays and turn into superbugs.

CHAPTER 6

Hot Spots

It was 2018. Civil war raged in Yemen. A young man came into a clinic. He had been hit by a bullet. His leg needed to be sewn up. Later, there was a bad smell. This showed he had an infection. The doctors did tests. They found bacteria. It was a superbug.

TAIZ, YEMEN

Doctors acted fast. The man was put in a room by himself. His family could not touch him. They wore masks and gloves during visits. Most antibiotics did not help. But the man was given something else. It was a drug of last resort. This saved his life.

The man was lucky. His medical team belonged to a special group. It was Doctors Without Borders. They came to Yemen for a reason. This country is a superbug hot spot.

DOCTORS WITHOUT BORDERS

Doctors Without Borders is an organization that sends doctors and nurses to places around the world that need help the most. These include war zones and other trouble spots.

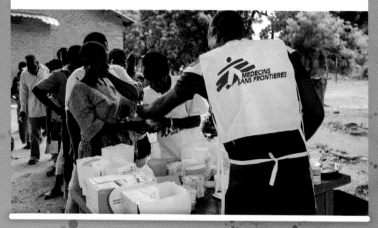

War Zone

The war in Yemen began in 2015. It wrecked the country's health-care system. Hospitals closed. Bombs went off. Shots were fired. Thousands were hurt. People lost limbs. Wounds were hard to keep clean. Water in the country was dirty. Pipes had been destroyed in the fighting. Infections spread quickly.

Clinics were set up. Many workers did not have training. But they did have one thing. It was antibiotics. These were cheap. There was a big supply. The clinics gave them out freely.

This saved many lives. But it caused a serious problem. Too many people took the drugs. Bacteria became resistant. Superbugs began to thrive.

Fighting Back

Doctors Without Borders runs a hospital in Yemen. It tracks superbugs. They test people who come in. Sixty percent have them. Each germ is tested. Then doctors pick the best drug to use.

There are other hot spots too. These are areas with many cases. The causes are often the same. Too many antibiotics are used. Hygiene is poor. War makes it worse. Poverty does too. Superbugs form. Then they spread.

No Place to Hide

Few spots are as bad as Yemen. But no country is safe from these bugs. Bugs do not care about borders. The world is connected. Trade goes around the globe. Goods sail across oceans. People fly from place to place. Germs travel with them.

Antibiotic overuse is not just in poor areas. Rich countries have a problem too. The U.S. is an example. People take too many of the drugs. Often, they are not needed.

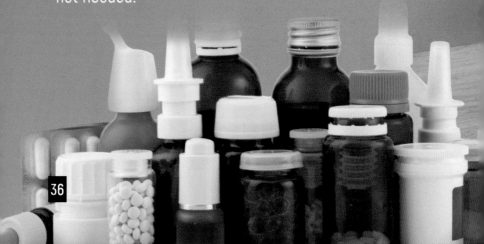

Too Many Drugs

This is a common scene. A patient goes to her doctor. She has a cough. "Doctor, will you give me an antibiotic?" she asks.

The doctor frowns. "Your illness is not that serious," he says. "It may be caused by a virus. An antibiotic will not help."

"Can you give it to me anyway?" the patient says. "I know it will make me feel better. Please?"

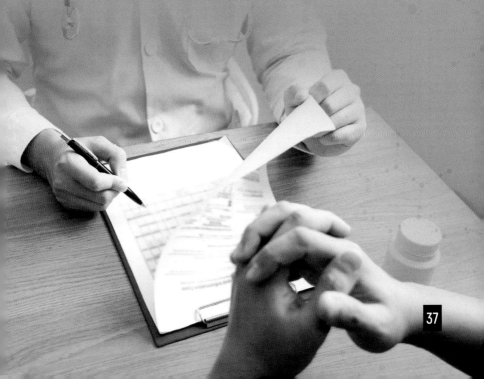

Doctors face tough choices. Patients worry. They make demands. It can be hard to say no. A doctor may give drugs that are not needed.

Once or twice may not hurt. But what if many doctors do this? The chance goes up that some bacteria will start to resist drugs.

SUPERBUG SUPERPOWERS

Superbugs do not only spread drug resistance to their offspring. They can also pass it to other bacteria. Many bacteria carry tiny packages called plasmids that contain genes, or instructions, to take on a trait. Some plasmids give special powers like drug resistance. A superbug can pass these plasmids on to other bacteria. This gives them the same power to resist drugs.

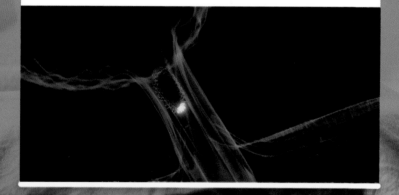

This is happening more often. Drugs are losing their power. Some could stop working entirely. This would be like turning back the clock. Everyday situations would be much more dangerous. A sore throat could turn deadly. Even having a baby might be a risk.

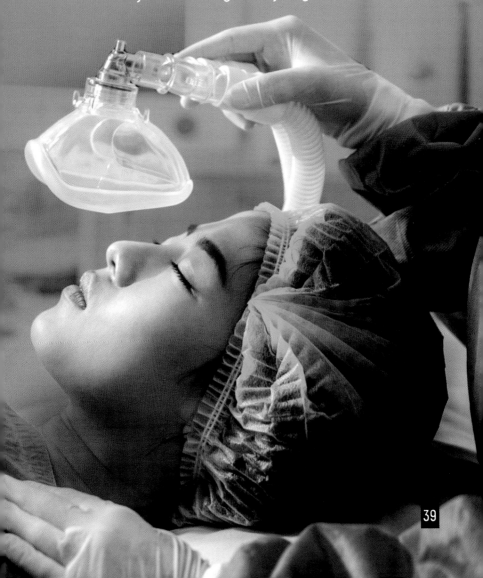

A Global Fight

One country cannot fight this alone. The threat is too big. All must work together. The United Nations has taken the lead. This is also called the UN. It represents nearly every country on Earth.

The UN gathered a group together. Scientists were called in. Leaders joined too. They drew up a plan. "No Time to Wait" is the title. It lays out steps to take. Amina Mohammed helped lead the project. "There is no time to wait," she explains. Superbugs are "one of the greatest threats we face."

FAST FACT: The United Nations was established in 1945. It brings together 193 countries to work on global issues such as health, peace, security, and human rights.

Group members set goals. One is to educate. People must learn about the problem. Another goal is research. For that, countries need money. This project helps raise it. Health-care workers are needed too. The UN sends them around the world. Drugs must be controlled. Setting rules helps. All of these steps add up. They can slow the spread of the bugs.

AMINA MOHAMMED

UNITED NATIONS

A COSTLY CRISIS

Superbugs could plunge 24 million people into extreme poverty by 2030. They could also cost the world economy $100 trillion by 2050. This would create a global financial crisis. Experts say it is much cheaper to take action now. By spending only $2 per person today, countries could do a great deal to prevent the crisis.

More Research

Science is also coming together. Labs across the world share their work on the web. One platform is called SPARK. This is a place to share findings. A team might make a discovery. It can be posted online. Another team across the world sees it. They can build on it. Many minds all work at once. This speeds up medical progress.

FAST FACT: SPARK stands for Shared Platform for Antibiotic Research and Knowledge. It is a cloud-based virtual laboratory. The goal of SPARK is to speed up the development of new drugs.

9

New Signs of Hope

Superbugs may be a few steps ahead. But science is catching up. Scientists have big plans. There are many ways to fight bugs. New drugs are just the start.

Dragon Blood

Scientists will look anywhere for a good idea. One place is in the mouth of a Komodo dragon. Bacteria live inside. Some are very harmful. But they do not hurt the dragon. Why not?

The answer is in its blood. A secret weapon lives there. It is DRGN-1. This fights the germs. Now scientists want to turn DRGN-1 into a drug.

Searching the Past

Early medicines came from plants. Today, some scientists are looking to the past for answers. They have searched old journals. These were from 1648. One told about a pepper tree. Its fruit was used to treat wounds.

Scientists found the tree in South America. They tested the fruit. The stories were true. It killed harmful bacteria. This could be a powerful medicine.

NATURAL ANTIBIOTICS

Plants are attacked by bacteria and fungi just like people are. Many plants produce chemicals that fight off these invaders.

Viruses to the Rescue

Would you give yourself a killer virus? Some people have. One virus kills bacteria. It is called a phage. First it lands on bacteria. Then it destroys them.

Using viruses this way is rare in the U.S. But a few Americans wanted to try it. They were superbug patients. Antibiotics did not work. Their options were running out. There was nowhere else to turn.

The patients got on a plane. They flew to Eastern Europe. Doctors gave them the treatment. It saved their lives. Now the U.S. is starting to use it.

FAST FACT: Phage is short for bacteriophage. That means "bacteria eater" in Greek.

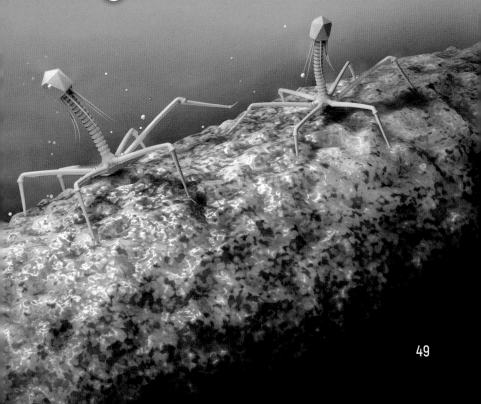

A Magnet for Germs

Superbugs spread in the body. They can also spread outside of it. Some stick to surfaces. A person might touch an object. Their hand picks up germs. Then they pass them to someone else.

Scientists came up with a fix. It is a new coating. This can cover objects. Germs are drawn to it. Then they are trapped. The coating kills 99 percent of them.

The Body's Fire Alarm

Our bodies fight germs. What if they got better at it? Scientists are looking for a way. They found something interesting. Our cells have their own "fire alarm." This is like a warning system.

Bacteria come in. Cells give off a chemical. This sends a message. It tells the immune system to attack. The finding gives scientists hope. They could create new drugs. These could make our built-in warning systems even better.

Staying Safe

Superbugs can be bad. But we are not powerless against them. We have many ways to stay safe. No special treatments are needed. A few good habits can go a long way.

The most important is to wash your hands. Hands pick up germs. They can spread them to others. Wash your hands often. Try not to touch your face. This includes the mouth, nose, and eyes. Germs can enter the body this way.

Eating a healthy diet can also help. This is one of the biggest ways to keep safe. The body can defend itself. But it needs vitamins. Vegetables provide them. Fruits do too. They keep the immune system strong.

Make sure meat is cooked well. Cooking kills many germs. Check the center of the meat. Is it still pink or red inside? That can be risky. Fruits and vegetables can also carry germs. Wash them thoroughly.

Some items should not be shared. Razors are one. Towels are another. Use your own. Do not borrow them from others. That can spread germs.

FAST FACT: In 2020, the COVID-19 global pandemic led many to worry about the creation of a new superbug. Due to secondary infections caused by the virus, many patients were being treated with antibiotics, which could lead to drug-resistant bugs.

Going Further

Some people want to do more than stay safe. They want to help stop superbugs. Many choose a career in science. Some become **microbiologists**. These experts study superbugs. Their goal is to find new treatments. It is an exciting field. This work can save lives.

The Future

Superbugs are a threat. Experts have warned us. The numbers are eye-opening. Millions of lives could be at risk. Doing nothing is not an option.

But there is hope. People around the world are rising to the challenge. Groups are forming. Governments have been taking action. Scientists make new discoveries each day.

Our world is more connected than ever before. This creates opportunities to work with one another. Beating superbugs will take a team effort. Together we can win.

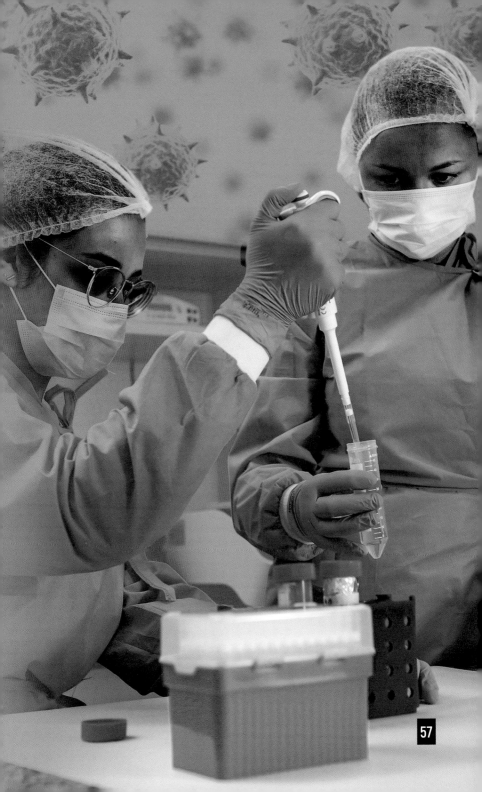

Glossary

adapt: to change to fit better into an environment

antibiotic: a medicine made to kill harmful bacteria

bacteria: very small living things

clinic: a place where people get medical help, sometimes for a lower cost than at a hospital

fungus: a living thing that looks like a plant but has no flower

hygiene: the things people do to keep themselves and the areas around them clean so that they have good health

immune system: the cells and organs that protect the body from infection

infection: an illness caused by a bacteria or virus

isolation: a place where infected patients can be kept separate from everyone else

microbiologist: a scientist who studies very tiny life forms such as viruses and bacteria

mold: a type of fungus with a fuzzy texture

mutate: to change DNA, resulting in new traits not normally found in a species

outbreak: the sudden spread of a disease

penicillin: a medication made from a mold that can kill bacteria

phage: a virus that copies itself by taking over a bacteria cell

positive: a test result showing that something is present

poverty: the state of not having enough money or resources

prevent: to stop something from happening

resist: to not be affected by something

virus: a very small molecule that takes over a cell in order to reproduce and can cause illness

TAKE A LOOK INSIDE

STEPHEN HAWKING

HIS LIFE AND LEGACY

CHAPTER

4

Turning Point

In 1962, Hawking entered Cambridge. He began his research in cosmology. The field covers big questions. How did the universe begin? What is it made of? How does it work?

Hawking was learning more about the world. Something else began to happen too. He was getting clumsy. Sometimes he would trip and fall. This happened more and more. One time was on the stairs. Another happened when he was ice skating. After a fall, Hawking could not get up. That seemed strange.

His mom took him to a doctor. They did tests. X-rays were done too. Muscle samples were taken from his arm. The doctors realized something was very wrong.

18

19

Diagnosis

Doctors told Hawking the news. His case was unusual. He had a disease. It was called ALS. This attacks the muscles. They stop working over time. People with ALS become paralyzed.

His doctors said there was no cure. It would just keep getting worse. Hawking might only have a few years to live. The news filled him with despair.

Then something happened to change his view. There was a young boy in the next bed at the hospital. He died of leukemia. Hawking realized something. Others had it worse than him. At least he was still alive. There was time left.

Hawking thought about his life. What if it was cut short? That meant every minute counted. Each day mattered. Then he made a decision. It was time to do some good while he still could.

FAST FACT: ALS stands for amyotrophic lateral sclerosis. It is also known as Lou Gehrig's disease. Lou Gehrig was a famous baseball player who got the disease in the 1930s.

ALS

ALS causes nerve cells in the brain and spinal cord to break down. The brain loses its ability to control muscles. In time, the muscles weaken and waste away.

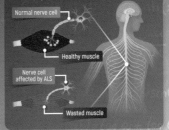

Normal nerve cell

Healthy muscle

Nerve cell affected by ALS

Wasted muscle

Secrets of the Universe

The book was popular for many reasons. Hawking made difficult ideas easy to understand. He posed big questions. How did the universe start? Where does it end? What is empty space made of? The answers were strange and wonderful.

Hawking showed that space is warped. Time can warp too. It passes at different speeds in different places.

The book explored whether aliens could visit. It told where stars come from. Stories were used to bring ideas to life.

A BRIEF HISTORY OF TIME FROM THE BIG BANG TO BLACK HOLES

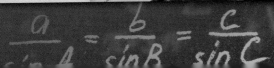

WHITE LIGHTNING BOOKS NONFICTION

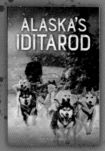
ALASKA'S IDITAROD

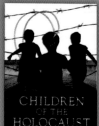
CHILDREN OF THE HOLOCAUST

CRYPTOCURRENCY

DEADLY BITES

DIGITAL WORLDS

DROIDS AND ROBOTS

ESPORTS

FLIGHT SQUADS

NAVAJO CODE TALKERS

OLYMPIC GAMES

STEPHEN HAWKING
HIS LIFE AND LEGACY

SUPERBUGS

THE WHITE HOUSE

WORKING DOGS

WORLD CUP SOCCER

MORE TITLES COMING SOON
SDLBACK.COM/WHITE-LIGHTNING-BOOKS